Explore

the World Christian Lifestyle

✦

**Discover how you can help reach those
unreached with the gospel**

ISBN: 978-1-947468-92-4

Published by Via Nations

PO Box 3556

Fayetteville, AR 72702

For more resources, visit vianations.org/resources

Translations

We desire to make this material available to as many as will use it around the world
in a way that honors everyone involved in the work. If you would like to translate or
adapt this resource to use in your cultural context, we are very open to collaborating
with you. There are guidelines for translators at vianations.org/translation.

Printed in Canada through Bookmark

Third Edition, First Imprint, 2023

C 10-5-22   M 2-28-23 11:01

Contents

Introduction

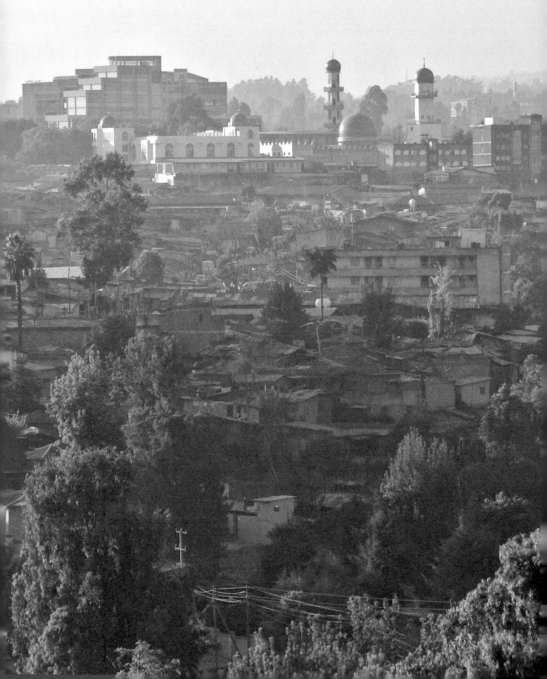

What is the Bible really about anyway? ✦ Is God still at work in the world today? ✦ Is my life meant to be part of something bigger?

WHAT IS *EXPLORE* ABOUT?

It is about God's promise to Abraham. ✦ It is about the passion of Jesus. ✦ It is about the purpose of the church. ✦ It is about a movement that is rapidly growing throughout the world. ✦ *It is about the very heart of God—His heart for the knowledge of His glory to cover the earth as the waters cover the sea (Hab 2:14).*

This study is designed to help you begin exploring God's Word, world, and work. So get together with some friends and talk about what you are learning on this journey!

HERE IS WHAT'S INVOLVED IN EACH OF THE SEVEN LESSONS:

✶ **Prep**   Evaluate your view of God's Word, world, and work.

▌ **Read**   Gain insight into what God is doing and how you can join Him.

❝ **Discuss**   Study the verses and express your thoughts in discussion with your *Explore* study group.

❧ **Live**   Examine new ways to live out your convictions.

⚱ **Pray**   Enter into God's presence and intercede for people groups who have not yet come to know and love Jesus.

THE WORLD CHRISTIAN SERIES

This study is designed to introduce what we call "World Christian Habits." World Christians are people who understand God's heart for the world and strategically live their lives in such a way that wherever they are and whatever they do, they are working to see Him glorified among all nations. Daily practices, such as praying, can be expanded into practical habits that we as Christians can implement in order to reach God's heart for other communities across the world. Other studies in the World Christian Series dive deeper into each particular habit. These habits include:

01   Praying   04   Going

02   Sending   05   Mobilizing

03   Welcoming

Ready to start exploring?

Lesson 01
GOD'S WORD

God's Heart *for the* World

> You can do something other than working with God in his purpose, but it will always be something lesser, and you couldn't come up with something better.
>
> —Steve Hawthorne

✳ Prep

From Genesis to Revelation

Many of us have grown up learning the Bible one story at a time, with each story applied directly to our personal lives in some way. How do you view and read the Bible?

01 **Rule book**
It tells me what to do and warns me about what not to do.

02 **Spiritual protection**
A verse a day keeps the devil away.

03 **Crystal ball**
It helps me know God's plans for my future, spouse, job, etc.

04 **Spiritual cup of coffee**
It helps me wake up and get the day started right.

05 **Family doctor**
I turn to it when I need something to make me feel better.

06 **Treasure map**
It reveals God's promises to bless me with health and wealth.

These are not all bad views, but the result is that many of us see the Bible as a random assortment of spiritual stories with no overriding theme or purpose. The reality is that the Bible is much more about God and His passion to be worshiped by all peoples than it is about us.

There are more than 1,600 verses throughout the Bible that show God's passion for His glory to be enjoyed by all peoples of the earth. This lesson highlights just a few of those verses. *For more verses, see the Biblical Basis of Missions section on page 090.*

Terms & Definitions

✦   **NATIONS**

In the Bible, this word most often refers to ethnic people groups. The words "peoples" or "Gentiles" are also used to convey the same idea.

✦   **WORLD CHRISTIANS**

People who understand God's heart for the world and strategically live their lives in such a way that wherever they are and whatever they do, they are working to see Him glorified among all nations.

◗ Read

God's Heart for the World

What verses come to mind when you think of the word, "missions?" Most of us are hard pressed to name more than the old faithful Great Commission. For years our church culture has singled out this passage to be the theme of our missions conferences and the motivation for those who go. It's no wonder that our obedience is slow — who wants to hang their future on one verse?

The Bible has a lot more to say on this subject than just the Great Commission. We need to understand the concept of a biblical basis for missions. Maybe you're saying, "The biblical basis — is there one?" Yes! In fact, God's desire for His glory to cover the earth permeates every book of the Bible. If you don't believe that all 66 books can be reduced to one theme, keep reading. You will see that missions is not your pastor's idea, or your campus minister's idea, or even your idea — it is God's. Since

creation, God has been intent on redeeming all peoples to Himself.

As Christians, it is vital that we see the world as He sees it. Let's look at the Bible in light of God's heart for the world, and we will see that from Genesis to Revelation, He is beckoning you, me, and all of His people to join Him in bringing every people group to His throne. The Bible is not a collection of separate books with no common theme or story. It is one book with one theme.

" Discuss

God's Global Passion and Purpose

The following verses are a sample of well known stories or passages with important global implications that are often missed. Once we are aware of God's global purpose, we start seeing the global thread throughout the Old and New Testaments. As you discuss, pay careful attention to the phrases and concepts that reveal God's global purpose. When you can, try to first answer the questions with phrases straight from the Scripture before adding your own commentary.

Our prayer is that these few verses will excite you to seek out more of the hundreds of passages in the global thread, as well as empower you to recognize and be convinced of this foundational biblical theme.

OVERVIEW

01 **A Foundational Promise: Genesis 12:1–3 & Galatians 3:8**
Discuss what God promised to Abram (soon to be called Abraham), God's intentions for Abraham and his descendants, and Paul's understanding of the gospel.

02 **An End Picture: Revelation 5:9–10 & Revelation 7:9–10**
What do these verses reveal about God's overall purpose and passion?

03   How do these verses inspire and encourage us?

_____

_____

_____

_____

OLD TESTAMENT

Though the Old Testament primarily deals with Israel, it is also filled with references about God's heart for all nations, and how His desire has always been for all nations.

01   **1 Samuel 17:45–47**
What was David's motivation for challenging Goliath?

_____

_____

_____

02   **1 Kings 8:41–43**
As Solomon prayed to dedicate the temple, what was his expectation of the Lord's fame and his desire for foreigners?

_____

_____

_____

03   **Daniel 6:25–27**
Right after Daniel was delivered from the lions, what was the result of his unyielding devotion to God?

_____

_____

_____

_____

04 **Psalm 67**

One third of all the Psalms have a direct reference to the nations and God's relationship with them. In this example, what stands out to you?

05 **Isaiah 49:6**

For further reference, see this verse quoted in Luke 2:25–32, referring to Jesus as the Messiah; and also Acts 13:46–48 as a command to Paul and Barnabas.

Israel thought that their Messiah was only for them and their benefit, but what does this verse teach us about the mission of the Messiah?

NEW TESTAMENT

01 **Matthew 28:18–20**

For further reference, see the other four commissioning statements: Mark 16:15, Luke 24:45–47, John 20:21, and Acts 1:8.

This verse is referred to as The Great Commission. Of all the things Jesus said and taught, why do you think He ended with this statement? How does this reflect God's global passion?

02 **Acts 17:26–27**

What do you learn in these verses about God's actions and desires toward all peoples throughout history?

03 **Romans 15:20–21**

Verse 21 is a quote from Isaiah 52:15.

Where did Paul seek to preach the gospel? Why did he have this ambition, and how did it fit in with God's desire for all the nations?

❧ Live

01 How has this lesson impacted the way you see God's Word and His global purpose and passion?

Ideas for living it out

01   Memorize three verses from this lesson that really impacted you.

02   To dig into more verses on God's global passion and purpose, take the 30-Day or 7-Day Challenge on the biblical basis of mission. You can find them at the bottom of page 091 in the resources section.

03   See if you can share this biblical basis of missions with another person or a group of people.

True Story

I really started growing spiritually in college. During my first summer, I attended a discipleship project, and we had a missions conference. I heard the guy up front say, "God's Word is not just a bunch of separate books. It's one book with one common theme throughout. God's glory will go out to all peoples on earth, and He wants you to be a part of it!" So I took the next couple of years and started diving into God's Word to truly see His heart for the world. I realized I needed to jump on board with what God is doing and is going to do. Soon after, I found out about an opportunity to go to India and share the gospel with high caste Hindus ... so I went!   — JOHN

01   What is one thing you want to do this week because of what you learned?

02   Who will keep you accountable?

⧗ Pray

Prayer is the privilege of every follower of Jesus Christ, no matter how old they are, where they live, or what they do for a job. Unfortunately, few believers pray the way Jesus taught us to pray. In Matthew 6:9–10, Jesus taught His followers to pray, "Father, hallowed be your name. Your kingdom come, your will be done on earth as it is in Heaven." Steve Hawthorne, global author and mobilizer, says about the Lord's Prayer:[1]

> This prayer is not a statement of praise. It is explicitly a request in the original language: "Father ... sanctify your name!" To paraphrase, "Father lift up, single out, exalt, manifest, and reveal Your name to the people of earth. Become famous for who You really are. Cause the people of earth to know and adore You!" The prayer can be prayed most thoroughly in the global dimension that Jesus taught: "on earth as it is in heaven."

How exciting to know that even right now we can join God in seeing His singular purpose and passion brought to fulfillment. In this section, we will pray for God's name to be hallowed among peoples of the earth who have little to no acccss to the gospel apart from a dream or vision.

Intercede

01 Father, we pray that you would indeed make your name holy and exalted among all the peoples of the earth. That your kingdom would come and your desires would happen on earth, among all peoples, the same way they happen in heaven.

02 God of heaven and earth, just like Abraham, David, Daniel, and Paul caught the vision for all the nations to know you, help me and all of your church to catch that same vision and live it out the way you want us to.

03 Father, you say that the harvest is plentiful, but the laborers are few; so we pray to you, the Lord of the Harvest, to send out laborers into your harvest fields!

Lesson 02
GOD'S WORLD

Religions *of the* World

> And this gospel of the kingdom will be proclaimed throughout the whole world as a testimony to all nations, and then the end will come.
>
> – Jesus

✳ Prep

The State of the World

In the last lesson, we saw God's promise to bless all ethnic peoples through Abraham and his descendants (us), and we saw the fulfillment of this promise in Revelation 7:9–10. Some natural questions would then be: "How close are we to seeing this promise fulfilled? What is left to do?"

Fact Check

Read together as a group and decide which are true and which are false.

Ⓣ Ⓕ In 100 AD, the worldwide ratio of unbelievers to believers was 360 to one. Today, one out of every 14 people are evangelical Christians.

Ⓣ Ⓕ Evangelical Christianity is the fastest growing religious movement in the world.

Ⓣ Ⓕ There are more evangelicals in Africa than in all of North America and Europe combined.

Ⓣ Ⓕ Worldwide, the Gideons hand out one million Scriptures every 4.5 days.

Ⓣ Ⓕ Many Muslims around the world are having dreams and visions of Jesus Christ.

Ⓣ Ⓕ In Islamic Indonesia, believers are nearing 15 percent of the population.

Terms & Definitions

✦ **PEOPLE GROUP/ETHNIC GROUP**
The largest group of people within which the gospel can spread as a church planting movement, without hitting barriers of understanding or acceptance (such as language, ethnicity, religion, culture, history, etc). Referred to as "peoples" or "nations" in the Bible.

✦ **REACHED PEOPLES**
People groups with a population of more than 2% indigenous (local) evangelical believers to evangelize and disciple the remaining non-believers.

✦ **UNREACHED PEOPLES**
There is no indigenous community of Christians with adequate numbers and resources to evangelize their own people (less than 2% evangelical).

Answers: Page 095

(T) (F) Between 85 and 95 percent of all believers who are serving as cross-cultural goers serve in already reached areas.

(T) (F) More than 30 percent of the world's 6,900+ languages need a written translation of the Bible.

(T) (F) There are more than 2.9 billion people in the world who have little or no access to the gospel.

(T) (F) About ⅓ of the world call themselves Christians, ⅓ are non-believers living in reached people groups, and ⅓ live in unreached people groups.

◆ Read

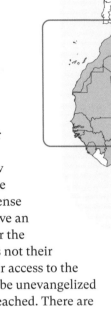

Those with No Access

If the command given by Jesus is to make disciples of all nations, then common sense tells us our job is to find those nations, or ethnic groups,[2] that have not been discipled (taught to be followers of Christ). If we want to fulfill the Great Commission, we need to know where these unreached groups of people are so that our efforts in completing the task will not just be busy, but productive.

The vast majority of these unreached people live in an area of the world nicknamed the "10/40 Window." The 10/40 Window is simply a term used to describe a region of the world within 10 and 40 degrees latitude from Western Africa to Eastern Asia. Of the more than 2.9 billion unreached people in the world today, about 97 percent live in the 10/40 Window. Less than 1 percent of these unreached people live in North and South America combined![3]

The 10/40 Window is a simple way to remember where the majority of the world's unreached people groups live. But it's important to remember that being unreached is less about a people group's location and more about their lack of access to the gospel.

Unreached people are not "more lost" than your neighbor or family member who does not know Christ. But, they are unreached in the sense that they do not have an opportunity to hear the gospel. The issue is not their "lostness," but their access to the gospel. People can be unevangelized without being unreached. There are people in the United States who have not heard the gospel, but they could if they wanted to. Most people living in the 10/40 Window couldn't find out about Jesus even if they wanted to!

Just imagine yourself as one of these people. There is no church you can attend on Sunday morning to hear the gospel. There are no bookstores where you can go to purchase a Bible. There are no Christians that you can go to and ask about their hope in Christ. In fact, you will live and die and never meet a Christian. And there is no mission effort focused on reaching you. You are living in a sea of people, as one among millions. You are utterly unengaged with the gospel. You have no access.

The issue is not lostness, but access to the gospel.

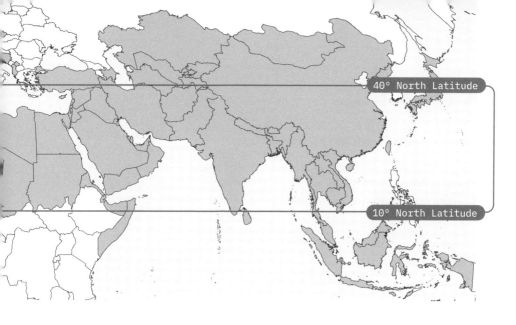

This area of the world remains un-reached for several reasons. First, these people do not live in a spiritual vacuum. The world's major religions began in this part of the world and are firmly entrenched there. In the 10/40 Window, there are about 1.3 billion Muslims, 860 million Hindus, and 275 million Buddhists.[4] Along with that, many of the countries in this region are oppressive to the spread of the gospel. However, Jesus declared that "the harvest is plen-tiful, but the workers are few." The biggest reason this part of the world is so unreached is because there is a lack of believers willing to go to these places.

It is estimated that less than 10 percent of foreign missionaries today are working to reach these unreached peoples. The other 90 per-cent are working in unevangelized, but not unreached, areas.[5] According to the World Christian Encyclope-dia, of all the money designated for "missions" in the United States, only two cents of every dollar is spent on reaching the unreached. The rest goes toward efforts to further evan-gelize reached people.

Martin Luther King, Jr. said, "Noth-ing in the world is more dangerous than sincere ignorance," and that proves true in our global strategies for advancing God's kingdom. We must take the time to educate our-selves on the state of the world and evaluate our efforts in line with God's command to make disciples of all people groups. We should celebrate all the advances that have been made in proclaiming the gospel through-out the world, while also taking on the challenge of reaching the people groups who are currently without access. Certainly this is a daunting challenge, but with God nothing is impossible, because this is what God has commissioned His church to do!

❝ Discuss

THUMB: Religions of the Unreached

As you have just read, most of the world's unreached people groups live in the 10/40 Window. An easy way to remember the major blocs of unreached peoples is the acronym THUMB (we'll explore each bloc further in the Pray sections).[6]

Tribal
161 million unreached people in 704 people groups
60 cross-cultural workers for every 1 million tribal people

Hindu
860 million unreached people in 1,843 people groups
2 workers for every 1 million Hindus

Unreligious
121 million unreached people in 15 people groups
12 workers for every 1 million unreligious

Muslim
1.3 billion unreached people in 1,344 people groups
6 workers for every 1 million Muslims

Buddhist
275 million unreached people in 227 people groups
13 workers for every 1 million Buddhists

01   What is your reaction to these statistics?

02   **John 4:35 & Matthew 9:37–38**
Also reference Luke 10:2
How does God view the world's potential to come to Him? What is His solution?

03   **John 3:16–18, 2 Thessalonians 1:6–10, Romans 6:23, & John 14:6**
What do these verses say about the reality of people living and dying without turning to Jesus? What will be your response to their situation?

04 **Habakkuk 2:14 & Matthew 24:14**

In light of the previous statistics about the unreached, what hope do these verses give us?

🌿 Live

01 How do these statistics compare with what you learned in Lesson 1 about God's heart for the nations?

02 How has this lesson caused you to see God's world in new ways?

Ideas for living it out

01 Check out websites focused on the unreached like joshuaproject.net, operationworld.org, peoplegroups.org, and prayercast.com. Specifically look at the THUMB prayer videos at joshuaproject.net/resources/ prayer_videos.

02 Start including prayer for the unreached as a regular part of your day — perhaps before meals, before bed, or at 10:40 every morning.

03 Share THUMB with three of your friends.

True Story
02

When I was 9, God placed the Mongolian peoples on my heart. While researching their country for a school project, I learned there were fewer than ten known believers in the entire country. I began to intercede daily, offering up simple prayers based on what I'd learned about the people and what I believed about God ... for Bibles to replace the Buddhist altars inside their tent homes ... for God to send believers to share the gospel with the three million Mongolians who had never heard the name of Jesus.

After two years of praying, a "Hope for Mongolia" article caught my eye. It described a movement of God in which 500 Mongolians came to know Jesus. I think this was God's way of telling me He was answering my prayers. — HOPE

01 What is one thing you want to do this week because of what you learned?

02 Who will keep you accountable?

⚡ Pray

Tribal Peoples

Tribal people live mostly in Africa, China, Southeast Asia, and Papua New Guinea.

BELIEFS OF TRIBAL PEOPLES

01 They have animistic and superstitious beliefs (everything has a spirit, such as water, rocks, trees, animals).

02 They must be careful not to offend these spirits and must appease them with sacrifices.

03 They often worship idols and ancestors and visit witch doctors.

Tai Dam (Black Tai) of Vietnam

825,000 people / 0.9% Evangelical

The Black Tai live along the banks of the Red and Black Rivers in northern Vietnam and are named for the color of the women's clothing. They are unusually polite, respectful, and hospitable. They are very sympathetic and full of humor, seeking any opportunity for feasting. The farming of wet rice dominates the economy. It is grown both as a dietary staple and for cash sales. Both the women and men plow, hoe, fish, cook, tend babies, clean house, and wash clothes.

The vast majority of the Black Tai practice ethnic religions. Theravada

Buddhism is mixed with folk animism, meaning that the people often seek help through supernatural spirits and objects. They practice ancestor worship (praying to deceased ancestors for guidance), and believe that there are spirits within every object and person. They also believe in "guardian spirits" and "locality spirits," which must be appeased so that they might avoid curses and receive blessings.

Intercede

01 God Most High, we pray that the Black Tai people would encounter your Holy Spirit and you would set them free from their bondage to all these other evil spirits.

02 Father, we pray blessing on the Black Tai's crops so they will seek you, the giver of all blessings. Also, we pray that they would find you as the true source of their compassion, joy, and hospitality.

03 Lord, in light of the statistics we read and the great need among the unreached, we pray for new funding and new missionaries to be raised up to focus on these precious people!

Lesson 03
GOD'S WORK

Praying
to the Lord *of*
the Harvest

" The man who mobilizes the Christian church to pray will make the greatest contribution to world evangelization in history.

—Andrew Murray

✳ Prep

Joining God's Global Mission Through Prayer

Our Father God has given us an amazing gift: intercessory prayer. Did you ever stop to think that your prayers work together with God's purposes to accomplish God's will? The Bible is full of stories of people who knew God's heart, prayed to God, and saw God move in powerful and dramatic ways! Let's join in God's mission and enjoy the adventure of intercessory prayer.

Fact Check

Read together as a group and decide which are true and which are false. After you check your answers, read the verses that go along with them.

Ⓣ Ⓕ As Christians, our struggle is primarily against people on this planet (Eph 6:12).

Ⓣ Ⓕ God will give us what we need as we ask according to God's will (1 John 5:14–15).

Ⓣ Ⓕ God desires all Christians to intercede for all people because He wants all people to be saved (1 Tim 2:1–4).

Ⓣ Ⓕ It delights your Father to give you His kingdom (Luke 12:32).

Ⓣ Ⓕ Jesus often got away from the crowds and His disciples so he could go pray (Luke 5:16).

Ⓣ Ⓕ Jesus, right now, is praying for us (Heb 7:25).

Terms & Definitions

✦ **INTERCEDING**

Praying to God on behalf of another person; taking up the cause and joining in the struggle of another by advocating for and pleading on their behalf.

(Answers: Page 095)

(T) (F) Prayer that truly effects change in circumstances is really only for the spiritual elite (James 5:16–18).

(T) (F) We are invited to come boldly before the throne of grace so we can find mercy and grace in our time of need (Heb 4:16).

(T) (F) Prayer is a significant response once we see the opportunity for mission and the current need (Matt 9:36–38, Luke 10:2)

❋ *What comes to mind when you think of prayer? What has your experience been with prayer?*

◆ Read

Praying God's Will and Seeing Change

Jesus commissioned His followers to "make disciples of all nations," and gave them the ministry of reconciliation. He said, "You will be my witnesses in Jerusalem, Judea and Samaria, and to the ends of the earth" (Matt 28:19, 2 Cor 5:18, Acts 1:8). Jesus knew that not all of us would be able to physically go to the ends of the earth and make disciples; however, He did expect us all to play our part. God empowered every believer with an amazing ability to join God in directly and dramatically effecting real change for "the ends of the earth." We call it prayer.

Most of the time, praying for God's kingdom to come in all the earth doesn't even cross our minds. If it does, it is often our last resort, something we pray out of obligation, or as a brief addition to our list of requests. All of these responses betray the fact that we do not really understand prayer or the power in our prayers that makes a specific and practical difference.

James tells us that "the prayer of a righteous person is powerful and effective" and gives us an example, saying that "Elijah was a human being, even as we are. He prayed earnestly that it would not rain, and it did not rain on the land for three and a half years. Again he prayed, and the heavens gave rain, and the earth produced its crops" (James 5:16–18). Now that is power! He was an ordinary human being, but he knew God's will, prayed earnestly, and God answered in power for all of Israel to see and give glory to God! How much more should prayer be the foundation of our relationship with God, since we have Jesus and the Holy Spirit living inside of us! Certainly James seems to think that this kind of prayer life should be more the norm than the exception for those who follow Jesus.

We are praying to
our Abba Father who
loves us, who wants a
relationship with us.

Paul tells us in Romans 8 that "the Spirit intercedes for God's people in accordance with the will of God," and that Christ Jesus "is at the right hand of God and is also interceding for [His children]" (Rom 8:26, 34; also see Heb 7:25). Since part of Jesus and the Holy Spirit's work is to intercede for believers, let's join with them in praying specifically for missionaries and God's work to reach the unreached. If we, like Elijah, learn to listen to God and learn to pray in agreement with Jesus and the Holy Spirit, then we will certainly be a vital part of bringing God's kingdom on earth "as it is in Heaven" (Matt 6:10).

Prayer also changes us. As we learn more of God's heart through prayer, He changes how we think and act. We learn to love the things He loves, hate the things He hates, and see things the way He sees them. For example, God significantly changed Peter through prayer. Acts 10:9 says, "about noon … Peter went up to the roof to pray." God spoke to Peter as he prayed, and Peter soon realized God's message—that "in every nation, anyone who fears Him and does what is right is acceptable to Him" (Acts 10:35). This radically changed Peter's perspective and ef-fectively changed the perspective of many in the church (Acts 10:45, 11:18, 15:14–19).

When we take a glimpse into the past, we see that prayer and missions movements are linked throughout history. The American mission movement was born in 1806 after five college students held a prayer meeting under a haystack while taking refuge from a thunderstorm. They discussed the spiritual darkness in Asia, every Christian's responsibility to do something, and then they prayed. As a result of that moment, those men dedicated themselves to the Great Commission and the "Haystack Prayer Movement" spread, sparking the creation of mission agencies which sent many Americans overseas to preach the gospel.

Jesus established this direct link between praying and going when He said, "The harvest is plentiful, but the laborers are few. Therefore pray earnestly to the Lord of the harvest to send out laborers into His harvest" (Luke 10:2). We must never disregard the power of this prayer or its need to continually be prayed. One could argue that so few have gone to the unreached because so few have obeyed Jesus' commandment to pray for laborers.

Lastly, we must remember who we are praying to and what we are praying for. This will give us confidence as we pray. We are praying to our Abba Father who loves us, who wants a relationship with us. He desires that no one be separated from Him, and sent His only son Jesus to purchase, with His own blood, a people for God (Rom 8:15, 2 Peter 3:9, John 3:16, Rev 5:9–10)! Our Father is passionate about reaching the lost and He loves to listen to and answer His children's prayers. Jesus tells us that if evil human beings know how to give good gifts to their kids, how much more does our Heavenly Father give "good gifts" and the Holy Spirit to His children when they ask (Matt 7:9–11, Luke 11:11–13)! "Ask and you will receive; seek and you will find; knock and the door will be opened" (Luke 11:9–10). This is how the kingdom of God works; this is the way of our Abba Father, our King!

“ Discuss

Paul truly believed that the prayers of Christians would change the current realities in his ministry. In each passage, what words, phrases, and concepts does Paul use in regard to people praying for him? What is Paul wholeheartedly relying on his supporters' prayers to do? Comment on anything else that jumps out to you.

01 **Romans 15:30–31**

02 **2 Corinthians 1:8–11**

03 **Ephesians 6:18–20**

05 **Colossians 4:3–4**

06 **2 Thessalonians 3:1–2**

In light of Paul's requests, if these things aren't happening with the Christian workers you or your church supports, perhaps the responsibility rests more on those who pray and send than on the workers.

❧ Live

01 What verses mentioned in this lesson (prep, read, and discuss sections) stood out to you? Are there other Bible verses on prayer that have impacted your thinking?

02 We all pray, but how often do we stop to listen to God impressing on us specific things to pray? Does this sound exciting or daunting?

Ideas for living it out

01   Pray daily for these great needs in reaching the unreached: more laborers going to the field, more resources focused on the unreached, and spiritual strongholds to be torn down among these groups (Luke 10:2, Eph 6:10).

02   Get one or all of these resources and use them to inform and guide you as you pray: Global Prayer Digest, Joshua Project app, prayercast.com videos, Operation World, or Window on the World.

03   Gather around a world map with photos and information about unreached people groups. Then find their location on the map and start praying.

"To know the will of God we need an open Bible and an open map."
—William Carey, pioneer missionary to India

True Story
（03）

While I was ministering in a country that was hostile to Christianity, I became frustrated because one of my local friends was very closed off to hearing about Jesus. I emailed my home church just before their Sunday service to pray for this person. The very next day, I saw my friend again and as we talked, I sensed a radical change had happened in her. She was not only open to talking about spiritual things, but really wanted to hear about Jesus. It was obvious that the dramatic change came as a direct result of my home church's prayers!   — TIM

01   How will you begin serving through prayer?

02   Who will keep you accountable?

⚡ Pray

Hindu Peoples

Hindus live mostly in India and Nepal.

BELIEFS OF HINDU PEOPLES

01   They believe in millions of gods.

02   They worship idols of their gods by giving them food, flowers, and money.

03   They believe they are caught in a cycle of birth-death-rebirth called reincarnation.

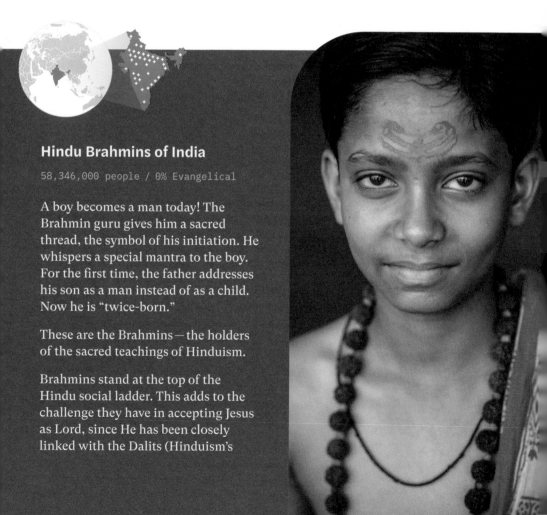

Hindu Brahmins of India

`58,346,000 people / 0% Evangelical`

A boy becomes a man today! The Brahmin guru gives him a sacred thread, the symbol of his initiation. He whispers a special mantra to the boy. For the first time, the father addresses his son as a man instead of as a child. Now he is "twice-born."

These are the Brahmins — the holders of the sacred teachings of Hinduism.

Brahmins stand at the top of the Hindu social ladder. This adds to the challenge they have in accepting Jesus as Lord, since He has been closely linked with the Dalits (Hinduism's

Untouchables). Brahmins have many barriers to the gospel of Jesus. Christ has a fellowship of all believers, but the Brahmin refuses to associate with an Untouchable. God offers eternal life, but a Brahmin believes he is on the verge of enlightenment, the perfect state of bliss that only comes after many reincarnations. In his mind, to accept Christ would mean losing it all.

Intercede

01   Father God, lead believers who can have influence in Brahmins' lives to reach out to them in all parts of the world. Holy Spirit, humble Brahmins so that they can receive your grace and your guidance.

02   Father of Lights, as the Brahmins seek enlightenment, open their eyes to the true light of the world, who is Jesus.

03   Father, you are willing that none should perish; give your church power to join you in praying for those who have never heard your Good News.

Lesson 04
GOD'S WORK

Sending Laborers *into the* Harvest Field

> " People who do not know the Lord ask why in the world we waste our lives as missionaries. They forget that they too are expending their lives … and when the bubble has burst they will have nothing of eternal significance to show for the years they have wasted.
>
> —Nate Saint

✴ Prep

No "A" Team and "B" Team

Given the verses in Lesson 1 and the stats in Lesson 2, we should all move to the 10/40 Window, right? Certainly, some should, but not all of us. Goers must have senders, and being a radical sender is just as important as being a radical goer.

Fact Check

Read together as a group and decide which are true and which are false.

(T) (F) Serving as a sender is just about giving money.

(T) (F) As long as we give 10 percent of our income to the church or missions, we are really free then to use the rest of our money however we want.

(T) (F) You can't be a sender until you have a good job.

(T) (F) Missionaries should not raise financial support because there are really no examples of anyone in Scripture living this way.

(T) (F) Taking care of those serving overseas in practical ways, such as sending them care packages, is not good to do since we don't want them to be dependent on us, but on God.

Terms & Definitions

✦   **SENDER**

People who leverage their career, money, skills, and influence to send and support others engaged in cross-cultural ministry.

Answers: Page 095

Ⓣ Ⓕ   Giving money is really more important than praying for missionaries and unreached peoples.

Ⓣ Ⓕ   Less than two cents of every dollar given to "missions" goes to take the gospel to the unreached.

✳   *When you think of a sender, what comes to mind?*

Read

Sending Well

Paul the Apostle has an interesting observation, "And how can they preach unless they are sent?" (Rom 10:15). The unreached do not have a chance at hearing the gospel if there are not people on the home front funding and praying for those that are going. It is like asking the question, "Which is more important—the rescuer who goes down into the well to save a life or the man at the top holding the rope?" You can't have one without the other.

In our culture we think we are entitled to live at whatever standard matches our income. When a person gets a raise, their standard of living gets a raise, too! But the World Christian should have a different mind-set. Maybe when a Christian gets a raise or comes into unexpected financial gain, God intends that person to be a resource for someone else! This thinking runs contrary to our culture.

A young married couple I know recently had a change of perspective and took responsibility for their role as senders. They read an article about creating your budget based on your giving priorities rather than on cultural expectations of how much

money you should spend on yourself. They had already been giving to missionaries, but felt that in light of God's desire for all nations, they needed to make this more of a priority. Unfortunately, due to circumstances in the next year, their income was cut in half. Yet because of their new focus on sending, they actually increased the total amount they gave from the year before!

Financial giving is a seemingly difficult habit for many people to develop because they always feel broke! But the point is not the amount that is given. The point is prioritizing all your resources, including finances, in light of God's kingdom.

The most obvious aspect of sending is giving of one's financial resources to support a missionary. But this is certainly not the only facet of sending. A sender may work in one or all of the following specialized roles: logistics, prayer coordination, communications, research, finances, or re-entry coordination. A specialist in logistics deals with the practical side of sending, like packing the missionary's goods, arranging travel plans, and acquiring items needed on the field. The prayer coordinator can

How can they preatch unless they are sent?

identify specific prayer needs based on research from missionaries in the field and missions agencies. They are also needed to enlist others in intercessory prayer for the team and organize special prayer meetings. For prayer needs to be circulated, a communications specialist is helpful. It is their responsibility to open the lines of communication from the field to the prayer team so that prayer requests and other needs are known. The role of sending is neither glamorous nor easy. The job of dealing with the day-to-day, behind the scenes tasks of mission work may seem thankless, but it is not without reward.

As a farmer's wife raising three small children, my grandmother faithfully handwrote a letter every week to all six overseas missionaries her church supported. Long before the ease of email communication, she saw the value in caring for and being a blessing to those serving so far away. For the missionaries, these letters were a reliable source of connection to home and a great encouragement. Also, whenever they were home on furlough, they stayed with her and were treated like royalty. She understood that sending is not only investing finances, but also giving practical care and regular encouragement.

For the gospel to be preached to all nations, the role of a sender is vital. As more Christians embrace this role, they enable greater and more effective missions efforts to the unreached.

Lastly, we must remember who we are praying to and what we are praying for. This will give us confidence as we pray. We are praying to our Abba Father who loves us, who wants a relationship with us. He de-

sires that no one be separated from Him, and sent His only son Jesus to purchase, with His own blood, a people for God (Rom 8:15, 2 Peter 3:9, John 3:16, Rev 5:9–10)! Our Father is passionate about reaching the lost and He loves to listen to and answer His children's prayers. Jesus tells us that if evil human beings know how to give good gifts to their kids, how much more does our Heavenly Father give "good gifts" and the Holy Spirit to His children when they ask (Matt 7:9–11, Luke 11:11–13)! "Ask and you will receive; seek and you will find; knock and the door will be opened" (Luke 11:9–10). This is how the kingdom of God works; this is the way of our Abba Father, our King!

❝ Discuss

01 **Romans 10:14–15**

What different roles are involved in getting the gospel to someone?

02 **Luke 8:1–3, Matthew 9:37–38, & Romans 15:30**

How was Jesus supported in His ministry? What were some ways people were asked to get involved?

03 **Psalm 24:1 & 1 Chronicles 29:14**

Where do our possessions come from? What do you think the difference is between ownership and stewardship?

04   **3 John 5–8**

In verse 6, what do you think it means to send in "a manner worthy of God?" In the last part of verse 8, what does John say is the relationship between sender and goer?

05   **Philippians 4:15–19**

What does Paul say happens when we serve as a sender?

06   **2 Corinthians 9:6–12**

What are some giving principles Paul is communicating here? How should we give? Why?

❧ Live

01   Make a list of three to 10 ways you could support cross-cultural missions, in addition to giving financially.

02   What are the obstacles you and those around you face in becoming a
      sender?

_____

_____

Ideas for living it out

01   Match whatever you spend on your "extras" (like eating out and
      entertainment) each month and give it to your church's cross-
      cultural goers.

02   Get on the mailing list of a cross-cultural goer and begin to pray for
      them daily.

03   Write an encouraging email to an overseas worker once a month.

True Story

I started supporting a friend who went to India for a year to share the gospel
with Hindu college students. Through giving, I really gained a heart for the
lost, and a strong desire to see the nations reached began to grow in me.
Supporting my friend allowed me to bless the nations and be a part of the
ministry in India. Sometimes it was hard because I just wanted to spend that
money on myself. But I stuck to my financial commitment, and it felt good to
spend my money in a way that put God's kingdom first in my life.

The Bible says that where your treasure is, there your heart will be also (Matt.
6:21). I wanted to invest my money in something more than myself that will
last for eternity!   — CELESTE

01   How will you begin to serve as a sender?

_____

_____

02   Who will keep you accountable?

_____

_____

⚡ Pray

Unreligious Peoples

Unreligious live mostly in China, North Korea, North Asia, and Europe.

BELIEFS OF UNRELIGIOUS PEOPLES

01   They are mostly atheistic, meaning they reject the belief or existence of deities.

02   Many have communist governments that tell the people there is no God

03   People groups being unreligious or atheistic is a recent development, mostly within the last 200 years.

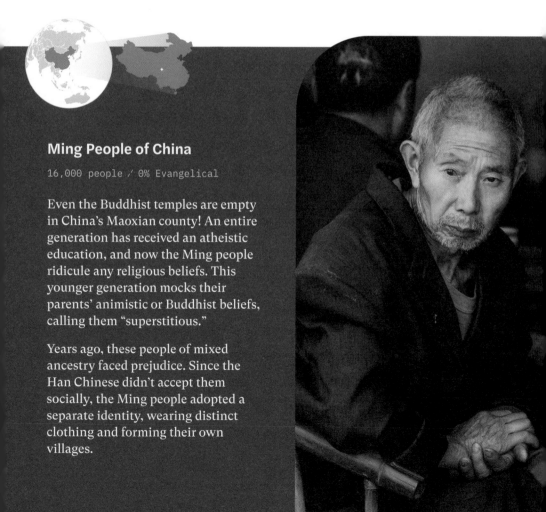

Ming People of China

16,000 people / 0% Evangelical

Even the Buddhist temples are empty in China's Maoxian county! An entire generation has received an atheistic education, and now the Ming people ridicule any religious beliefs. This younger generation mocks their parents' animistic or Buddhist beliefs, calling them "superstitious."

Years ago, these people of mixed ancestry faced prejudice. Since the Han Chinese didn't accept them socially, the Ming people adopted a separate identity, wearing distinct clothing and forming their own villages.

Teams of Christians who try to distribute gospel literature face arrest. Will the more than 15,000 Ming people living in this region ever hear of salvation through Christ?

Intercede

01 Father, you know the Ming have been oppressed and faced discrimination. Reveal to them that in Christ they are loved, valued, and accepted. Show them their place in your family

02 God of love, speak your love over the anger in many Ming people's hearts. Bring healing to them and open their hearts to receive the truth about who you are.

03 Father, help your people worldwide evaluate their time and resources in light of your Great Commission. Help us all respond with joy and open hearts so we can send out more laborers.

Lesson 05
GOD'S WORK

Welcoming *the* Nations Among Us

> " I am ready to burn out for God. I am ready to endure any hardship, if by any means I might save some. The longing of my heart is to make known my glorious redeemer to those who have never heard.
>
> —William Burns

✳ Prep

In Our Backyard

God is bringing college students, professionals, and families to the U.S. from people groups with little or no direct access to the gospel. Many of these internationals are the best and brightest from their countries, and many of them are living right in our dorms and neighborhoods. However, some are refugees who have been permanently displaced and relocated to our country, often in need of great help. In this lesson we will see God's heart for those who are away from their homelands and how He wants us to extend His love in tangible ways.

Fact Check

Read together as a group and decide which are true and which are false. After you check your answers, read the verses that go along with them.

(T) (F) Welcoming internationals is only for people who have the gift of hospitality.

(T) (F) There are more than 1 million international students who study and live in the United States each year.

(T) (F) Many internationals believe all Americans are Christians.

(T) (F) Most internationals don't even really have time to be friends with Americans.

(T) (F) The majority of internationals will never be invited into an American home.

(T) (F) 60 percent of international students come from the 10/40 Window.

Terms & Definitions

✦ **WELCOMER**
One who welcomes internationals into the culture by initiating relationships with them, showing hospitality, and sharing the love of Christ.

✦ **INTERNATIONALS**
Students, professionals, refugees, and families who are living in a country other than their homeland.

Answers: Page 095

(T) (F) Many internationals will return to their home countries to be leaders in business, education, and politics.

(T) (F) To really be an effective welcomer to internationals, you have to have a lot of time, money, personal charm, and discussion topics ready at hand.

✳ *What comes to mind when you think of internationals? What scares you the most about reaching out to students or families from other countries?*

◗ Read

The Nations Among Us

We live in a far different world than our parents or grandparents did. Globalization has ushered in a new era in which people across the world are increasingly mobile and interconnected. As the church, we cannot ignore these trends as we work to carry out Jesus' command to make disciples of all nations. It forces us to evaluate the most strategic way to move forward in reaching all nations with the gospel. In light of current global trends, an increasingly effective way to reach the nations is by welcoming internationals, or engaging them through friendship and hospitality to share the love of Christ.

In the past, students rarely left their home countries to study abroad. That was a privilege reserved only for the wealthy. But this is no longer the case. Students now cross oceans to seek out educational and vocational opportunities in dozens of fields. While more than 1 million international students are studying in the United States alone, this is not just a western phenomenon. When I was living in Russia, I was surprised at the number of Chinese, Turkish, and African students who migrated to Russia for their education.

This is an unparalleled moment in history. More than half of the internationals who come to study in the U.S. are from countries in the 10/40 Window, and many are from unreached people groups. The nations we pray for and endeavor to reach with the hope of the gospel are now among us in astounding numbers.

Whether they travel to New York City, Beijing, or Nairobi, international students spend anywhere from six months to six years studying abroad at a university. After this, many re-

International students
spend most of their
time isolated from
their host culture
This is a missed
opportunity for the
church.

turn to their home countries to begin their professional careers. What if they could be won to Jesus Christ and trained as disciples during their college years? They would then return to their homes — back to China, India, or the Middle East — not just with an education, but as ambassadors for Christ.

We might call this strategy "missions in reverse." Internationals already know their language and culture. When they return home, they re-enter established social and relational networks. They have existing spheres of influence waiting for them in their country. We can help reach the nations by equipping these students to reach their own people.

Unfortunately, statistics show that most international students spend their time abroad almost completely isolated from their host culture. Few are invited into our homes as guests. One survey showed that 80 percent of international students in the U.S.

never see the inside of an American's home — the very experience they wish for most. I suspect this trend remains true in other cities around the world where foreign students study. This is a missed opportunity for the Christian church today!

Though it might not initially seem so, internationals are really just like us. They miss their homes and their families. They experience loneliness, culture shock, and sometimes depression. It makes all the difference when believers step out to initiate relationships with them. One of their greatest needs is for friendship and someone to help them navigate through a foreign culture.

There is nothing complicated about being a welcomer. It starts with just making a friend. Imagine a wave of indigenous ambassadors of Jesus Christ flowing back to their nations from universities across the world — it all starts when the church welcomes them.

The nations are here. The opportunity to impact the world for Jesus Christ is waiting right outside our doors. Let's embrace the opportunity to welcome them into our homes and churches.

" Discuss

01 **Leviticus 19:34 & Deuteronomy 10:18–20**

What do these verses reveal about God's heart for internationals? What would it look like to "love them as yourself?"

02 **1 Kings 8:41–43, Isaiah 56:6–7, & Mark 11:17**

How does God feel about the prayers of "foreigners?" How can we see internationals as precious people created in the image of God, and not as projects?

03 **Acts 1:8, 8:27–31, 35–39**

In light of Jesus' commands here, how could it be strategic to reach out to internationals who are in our country?

04 **Mark 5:14–20 & John 4:39–42**

What can we learn from these passages about Jesus' attitude toward foreigners? How did one person's encounter with Jesus impact the entire community?

05 **1 Thessalonians 2:7–8**

What can we learn from Paul's example of sharing not only the gospel with others, but also his life? How might this relate to our outreach to internationals?

❧ Live

01 How have your thoughts about internationals changed after examining God's Word on the topic?

Ideas for living it out

01 Initiate a conversation with the next international you see (this will likely be more awkward for you than for them). Introduce yourself and

ask questions about their culture. After your conversation, ask if they would like to get together to talk more. Get their number and you are on your way.

02 Go to the university recreation facility, international restaurants, or grocery stores to meet new international friends.

03 Invite your new friend(s) into whatever you are doing (laundry, shopping, studying, going home for a holiday break).

True Story

I met Samuel, a Chinese international student, after I came back from a short-term trip to China. We started getting together to play basketball and eat meals. One day over lunch, Samuel asked if he could go to church with me. I excitedly agreed. Samuel started asking me questions about the Bible, and I tried my best to answer him and show him God's Word.

One day while we were hanging out, I felt God leading me to explicitly share the gospel with him. Samuel understood and accepted Christ that night!

All it took for me to welcome an international was to be available and obedient. I didn't do anything. I was just along for the ride while God was accomplishing His purpose through me! —HUDSON

Hudson was great! It was really his attitude and personality that drew me to Christ. I remember him inviting me to hang out all the time. Almost every night we did something. And every time I had a question about the Bible or Jesus, Hudson always helped me find an answer. I'm really thankful Hudson is my friend. —SAMUEL

01 How will you begin to serve as a welcomer?

02 Who will keep you accountable?

⚊ Pray

Muslim Peoples

Muslims live mostly in North Africa, the Middle East, and Indonesia.

BELIEFS OF UNRELIGIOUS PEOPLES

01   They believe in one god, named Allah, and that Muhammad was his final prophet.

02   They believe if the good deeds done in life outweigh the bad deeds when they die, they go to paradise.

03   They respect Jesus as a good prophet, but do not believe He is God.

Baggara, Messiria of Sudan

609,000 people ⁄ 0% Evangelical

Most of the Baggara are nomadic herdsmen in northern Sudan and the surrounding region. The Baggara live in simple dome-shaped tents that are arranged in a circle, which the cattle are brought into for the night. The Baggara tribes are almost completely Muslim, faithfully observing the "five pillars of Islam." Many of the men and some of the women are able to make pilgrimages to Mecca.

In each village, a council of men are the decision makers, and all men are involved with caring for the herds. The minority that live in farm communities also plant and harvest the crops. The Baggara are somewhat unusual in that the women work to provide the income needed to maintain the households. They earn cash by milking the cows and selling the milk or milk products. A married woman owns the tent, as well as all of its housekeeping contents.

Very little evangelization has been done among the Baggara tribes. The New Testament has been translated into their language, and some Christian broadcasts are also available to them. However, because the people are so devoted to the Islamic faith, very few Baggara have converted to follow Jesus. In addition, the nomadic lifestyle of many of the Baggara makes it difficult for missionaries to reach them.

Intercede

01 Though the Baggara people are nomadic, may they find their spiritual home and rest in you, Father. We pray for them to know you as the Good Shepherd and follow your voice.

02 Lord, please open my eyes and connect me to international students who are searching for truth and are eager to learn about you.

03 Father, give me courage to be intentional in welcoming and building relationships with the internationals I meet.

Lesson 06
GOD'S WORK

Going Where *the* Church Is Not

> Some wish to live within the sound of a
> chapel bell; I want to run a rescue shop
> within a yard of hell.
>
> —C.T. Studd

✳ Prep

To the Ends of the Earth

In Lesson 2, we saw that there are many people groups who have little to no access to the gospel. We need more of God's people who will give their lives to serve as cross-cultural servants among unreached peoples. God can use any one of us, with whatever skills, talents, abilities, vocations, or personalities we bring to the table, to minister among the unreached of the world.

Fact Check

Read together as a group and decide which are true and which are false. After you check your answers, read the verses that go along with them.

(T) (F) Those who are cross-cultural goers need to be gifted linguists.

(T) (F) You should not even consider going as a cross-cultural worker if you have student debt.

(T) (F) Most cross-cultural goers cannot use their degrees, or job experience.

(T) (F) To serve as a cross-cultural goer, you must be a church planter or English teacher because that is pretty much all there is to do overseas.

(T) (F) If your family doesn't want you to go overseas, you should stay home no matter what.

Terms & Definitions

✦ **CROSS-CULTURAL GOER**
One who is laboring to reach people of a significantly different culture than their own with the truth of Jesus. Most often, this is on a foreign or distant "field."

✦ **FRONTIER GOER** ,
Cross-cultural worker that seeks to establish communities of indigenous believers within people groups where the church does not yet exist.

Answers: Page 095

Ⓣ Ⓕ You should not go overseas as a cross-cultural goer if you are not married.

Ⓣ Ⓕ God will not lead someone who desires to go as a cross-cultural laborer to dangerous or hard places.
If you want to go somewhere like this, it cannot be God's leading.

Ⓣ Ⓕ If you haven't raised support or don't like to do it, then going probably is not for you.

✱ *What comes to mind when you think of a missionary? What scares you most about the thought of serving God as a cross-cultural goer?*

◗ Read

A Missionary Call

What constitutes a missionary call? It is a good sign that men ask this question. First, because it suggests that they think of the missionary enterprise as singularly related to the will of God. Second, because it indicates that they believe their lives are owned by a Person who has a right to direct them and whose call they must await.

But when we have said these two things, I think we have said everything that can be said in favor of the question because, far too often, it is asked for thoroughly unchristian reasons.

For instance, Christians will pursue a profession here in the United States having demanded far less positive assurance that this is God's will than it is for them to go out into the mission field. But by what right do they make such distinctions? Christianity contends that the whole of life and all services are to be consecrated; no man should dare to do anything but the will of God. And before he adopts a course of action, a man should know nothing less nor more than that it is God's will for him to pursue it.

If men are going to draw lines of division between different kinds of service, what preposterous reasoning leads them to think that it requires less divine sanction for a man to spend his life easily among Christians than it requires for him to go out as a missionary to the heathen? If men are to have special calls for anything, they ought to have special calls to go about their own business, to have a nice time all their lives, to choose the soft places, to make money, and to gratify their own ambitions.

With many of us it is
not a missionary call
at all that we are
looking for; it is
a shove.

There is a general obligation resting upon Christians to see that the gospel of Jesus Christ is preached to the world. You and I need no special call to apply that general call of God to our lives. We do need a special call to exempt us from its application to our lives. In other words, every one of us stands under a presumptive obligation to give his life to the world unless we have some special exemption.

This whole business of asking for special calls to missionary work does violence to the Bible. There is the command, "Go ye into all the world and preach the gospel to every creature." We say, "That means other people." There is the promise, "Come unto Me all ye that labor and are heavy laden and I will give you rest." We say, "That means me." We must have a special divine indication that we fall under the command; we do not ask any special divine indication that we fall under the blessing. By what right do we draw this line of distinction between the obligations of Christianity and its privileges? By what right do we accept the privileges as applying to every Christian and relegate its obligations to the conscience of the few?

It does violence to the ordinary canons of common sense and honest judgment. We do not think of ordering other areas of our lives on this basis.

If I were standing by the bank of a stream, and some little children were drowning, I would not need an officer of the law to come along and serve on me some legal paper commanding me under such and such a penalty to rescue those children. I should despise myself if I should stand there with the possibility of saving those little lives, waiting until, by some legal proceeding, I was personally designated to rescue them!

Why do we apply, in a matter of infinitely more consequence, principles that we would loathe and abhor if anybody should suggest that we should apply them in the practical affairs of our daily life? Listen for a moment to the wail of the hungry world. Feel for one hour its sufferings. Sympathize for one moment with its woes. And then regard it just as you would regard human want in your neighbor, or the want that you meet as you pass down the street, or anywhere in life.

There is something wonderfully misleading, full of hallucination and delusion in this business of missionary calls. With many of us it is not a missionary call at all that we are looking for; it is a shove. There are a great many of us who would never hear a call if it came. Somebody must come and coerce us before we will go into missionary work.

Every one of us rests under a sort of general obligation to give life and time and possession to the evangelization of the souls everywhere that have never heard of Jesus Christ. And we are bound to go, unless we can offer some sure ground of exemption which we could with a clear conscience present to Jesus Christ and be sure of His approval upon it.

"Well," you ask, "do you mean, then, that I should take my life in my own hands?" No! That is precisely what I am protesting against! That is exactly what we have done. We have taken our lives in our own hands and proposed to go our own way unless God compels us to go some other way. What I ask is that, until God reveals to us some special, individual path on either side, we should give our lives over into Jesus' hands to go in that path which He has clearly marked out before His church.

" Discuss

01 **2 Corinthians 5:18–20**

What has God given to all Christians? What has He called us all to be and do?

02 **Revelation 5:9 & 2 Peter 3:9**

When you think of "people who are lost," who do you think of and how does that affect you? Who do you think comes to God's mind when He thinks about the "lost" and how do you think it affects Him?

03   What do you think are some of the top reasons people give for not being a missionary? Are they reasons or excuses?

04   **Romans 15:19b–21**

In lesson two we learned that only about 10% of goers are among unreached people groups. Why should Paul's ambition be the aim of more cross-cultural goers? How is this essential to seeing God's global purpose completed?

05   **Romans 10:13–15**

Based on these verses, what is needed and why is it essential?

❧ Live

01   Many of Jesus' first disciples preached and were martyred anywhere from 1,200 to 3,100 km away from Jerusalem. They traveled as far as southern Ethiopia, most of northern Africa, throughout the Roman Empire, up to the British Isles, across Arabia, into Persia and even India! In light of their sacrifice, think through what you are willing to sacrifice to see the gospel preached globally.

02   What is stopping you from committing your life to seeing an unreached people group come to worship Jesus?

Ideas for living it out

01   Go on a strategic short-term trip within the next year.

02   Confess daily to God that you will go anywhere, at anytime, to do anything for Him, and then be open to His leading.

03   Find someone who is or was a long-term cross-cultural goer and ask to hear his/her story.

True Story

We heard about God's heart for the nations at a World Christian Seminar, and learned about the statistics of those who don't have access to Jesus. The information made us take stock of our lives. We had just bought our first home, had jobs we loved, and just had a baby. But we couldn't point to anything in our lives that reflected God's desire to be known among the nations.

Twenty months after our initial encounter, we were leaving for East Asia with our two-year-old and our nine-month-old baby. Most people thought we were crazy, some thought we were heroes, but we knew we were merely willing to obey. After twelve years of fruitful ministry and adding four more kids (three adopted), we moved our family to Africa. We wouldn't choose anything different because no earthly pleasure can touch the satisfaction of knowing we have followed Him to where the strategic need is the greatest. — SEAN AND AMANDA

01   How will you begin to serve as a welcomer?

02   Who will keep you accountable?

⧖ Pray

Buddhist Peoples

Buddhists live mostly in Southeast Asia, China, and Japan.

BELIEFS OF UNRELIGIOUS PEOPLES

01   They believe that suffering is caused by desire.

02   To end suffering, they must rid themselves of desire through meditation and multiple reincarnations.

03   The ultimate goal is to reach nirvana, where suffering ends and the self ceases to exist.

Bumthangpa People of Bhutan

```
23,000 people / Less than 0.6%
Evangelical
```

Bhutan is a Buddhist kingdom located in the Himalayan Mountains and its name means "Land of the Thunderdragon." The Bumthangpa have been living in the central Bhutan valley of Bumthang since before the 7th century. Bumthangpa are agrarian and their practices consist largely of subsistence farming (mostly rice and buckwheat) and animal husbandry (including cattle, sheep, and yak). Hundreds of people walk to the weekly market in Jakar to buy and sell food and supplies. In fact, the Bumthangpa have lived in almost the exact same way for more than 1,200 years.

Their religious practices have also not changed. They practice a form of Buddhism that incorporates the worship of local deities, which requires daily incense burning to household and local gods. Monks are the community leaders, and every aspect of a Bumthangpa person's life is shaped by Buddhism; the monks are even responsible for naming all the children. Interestingly, in one of their annual religious festivals, the monks go throughout the village and cast out the spirits who cause harm. Then the whole village gathers together and people run through a 10-foot-high arch of fire in order to purify themselves for the new year.

Intercede

01 Most High God, reveal to the Bumthangpa people that the only way to deal with suffering is through the peace and life of Jesus Christ. Reveal Jesus to these people in powerful and life changing ways.

02 Father, show these people that only you have the power to truly deliver them from evil spirits and purify them from their sins.

03 Lord of the harvest, we ask you to empower and send out a new wave of laborers to the unreached and the hard places of the world, like Bhutan and the Bumthangpa people.

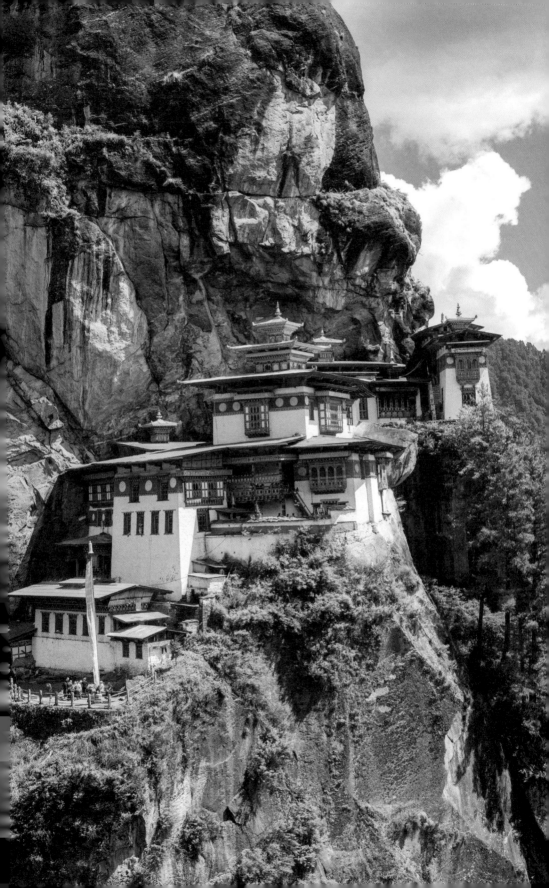

GOD'S WORK

Mobilizing *the* Body *of* Christ

66 Expect great things from God. Attempt
great things for God.

—William Carey

✳ Prep

Calling Others to Action

For the last six lessons, we have looked at the biblical basis for God's global purpose, seen what is left to fulfill, and examined four World Christian practices: praying, sending, welcoming, and going. This last lesson is focused on the fifth practice: mobilizing. You have been blessed, and now it is time to pass on the blessing to others.

Fact Check

Read together as a group and decide which are true and which are false. After you check your answers, read the verses that go along with them.

Ⓣ Ⓕ You have to be outgoing to be a mobilizer.

Ⓣ Ⓕ Mobilization is found in the Bible.

Ⓣ Ⓕ You must be formally trained to mobilize.

Ⓣ Ⓕ Mobilization is only sharing facts; no one wants to hear your story.

Ⓣ Ⓕ Mobilization is trying to get everyone to live in another country.

Ⓣ Ⓕ Only one person out of every 100 people interested in being a cross-cultural goer actually fulfills a long-term assignment.

Ⓣ Ⓕ Mobilizing is hard because there are not many resources available.

Terms & Definitions

✦ **MOBILIZERS**
People who empower others with global vision, passion, and strategy, helping them get personally connected to finding their most strategic role in the Great Commission.

✦ **WORLD CHRISTIANS**
People who understand God's heart for the world and strategically live their lives in such a way that wherever they are and whatever they do, they are working to see Him glorified among all nations.

(Answers: Page 095)

(T) (F) Mobilizers are those who pray, go, send, and welcome, while inviting others to join them.

✱ *What do you think of when you think about mobilization? How are these things related to God's heart to reach all nations?*

▪ Read

Modeling and Inviting

Have you ever been really excited about something, or loved something so much that you had to tell others about it? Perhaps it was a movie, a new electronic device, a vacation spot, or a hobby. Whatever you love, you tell others about. You want them to be just as excited as you are. In your enthusiasm, did you ever convince someone else to buy your favorite product, see the movie, or join in your hobby? If so, congratulations; you mobilized them!

Just like we feel joy when people share in our excitement, God experiences joy when we are excited about the things that delight His heart. Our Father is passionate about reaching out to those who have never heard the gospel, and He loves when we join Him in that excitement. Mobilizing people to the unreached is simply sharing God's excitement, and ours, in such a way that people are compelled to join God's mission and grow into a World Christian lifestyle.

Mobilizers are World Christians who help other believers become World Christians. They take people from being spectators of God's global mission to being active participants, living out their most strategic role in the Great Commission. Through mobilization, we point believers around the world to entire people groups who have no access to the gospel.

The best way to raise up other World Christians is to first model the lifestyle, and then invite others to join you. As you pray for the nations, invite someone to pray with you. As you financially support and send encouraging notes to missionaries, invite someone to give and write notes too. As you welcome someone from a different culture and religion into your life, invite a friend to welcome internationals along with you.

Jesus is our example in modeling and inviting. He lived a life of intentionality and purpose, and then invited others to do the same. Since modeling and inviting is the very heart of mobilization, all of us can be mobilizers. Whether we are business professionals, stay-at-home moms, or students; whether we are young, old, or middle-aged; whether we are very outgoing or more reserved—we can all find a way to model the World

Mobilizers help other believers become World Christians.

Christian lifestyle and invite others to join us.

If you already pray before meals, how about including a missionary or an unreached people group in that prayer? How about asking others to do the same thing and equipping them with resources to pray effectively? If you already are in a Sunday school class or small group, consider asking if your group could spend some time on the biblical basis of missions and status of the world. If you already read and discuss world news, how about sharing with people how current events are affecting unreached people groups? If you already eat out with friends, try going to an ethnic restaurant regularly and befriending the staff. These are just a few ways to exert World Christian influence to those around you. Certainly these activities will push you out of your comfort zone, but as you are intentional about giving priority to God's global mission, the habit of modeling and inviting will become a part of who you are and what you do.

If you help just one person a year become a World Christian, you are a mobilizer. If you help 10 people, or 50, or 500, you are a mobilizer. Mobilization can take different forms, but often a good place to start is taking people through the same process you went through in becoming a World Christian. The important thing is to seek the Lord, make a plan, and be intentional.

Here are three things to remember as you mobilize:

01 **Mobilizers are relational.** It's most effective when we connect with people life-on-life. We could simply inform people what they should do to grow into a World Christian lifestyle, but it is better if we walk with them through the process. Be intentional and available to answer questions. Help them overcome fears and encourage them as they grow.

02 **Mobilizers utilize resources.** We direct people to resourc-

es that help them develop as World Christians. Whether it is a missions book, short video, missions agency, prayer materials, or a website, seek to be knowledgeable about available resources. You don't need to know all the information, just know where to find it. Check out the Appendix on page 088 to get started.

03 **Mobilizers are humble.** We are not here to tell churches, pastors, or people that they are wrong or they are not doing enough. We are here to encourage, inspire, and model a lifestyle of participation in the Great Commission. Mobilizers should be a blessing to a local church. If possible,

work your mobilization plan within your local body with your leaders' blessing and input, as well as everywhere else that God opens a door.

Regardless of where you think mobilization might lead you, I invite you to start somewhere. The same Spirit that raised Jesus from the dead lives in you! And the same Spirit that empowered the early church to be Jesus' "witnesses in Jerusalem, Judea and Samaria, and to the ends of the earth" lives in you (Acts 1:8)! God loves all the people of the world, and He is eager to empower you in getting more people to join His great mission. I invite you to make mobilization part of your lifestyle. I invite you to go mobilize.

" Discuss

01 What are your thoughts and feelings about mobilizing others? Are you excited, scared, unsure, confident, etc.?

02 **Matthew 4:19 & 1 Corinthians 11:1**
What do these verses reveal about how Jesus and Paul mobilized God's people? What then are the implications for our lives?

03   **Luke 24:45–48**
In light of what we learned in lesson one, how did Jesus model mobilization in these verses? What did Jesus want the disciples to understand?

04   **Matthew 9:36–38 & Luke 10:1–2**
In light of lesson two, how did Jesus model mobilization in these verses? How does Jesus describe the lost versus the laborers? What practical actions did Jesus promote?

05 **Romans 10:14–15**

What roles do you see in this passage? How does mobilization fit into the passage and these roles?

06 **Revelation 5:9, 7:9–10**

These were two of the first verses we read in *Explore*. Reflecting on them now, what are your thoughts? How could you use these two verses to mobilize?

❧ Live

True Story   ⑦

When I caught the vision of God's heart for the world, I really began to see the need in the 10/40 Window and among the unreached. I wanted to empower others to get involved, so I started sharing verses about God's heart for the world in my Bible study. I also invited the other girls in my study to come with me as I met new international friends. The girls really caught the vision to reach the nations and have started passing it on to others. It is so great to see God influencing and mobilizing His church to take the gospel to the ends of the earth! — JENNIE

Ideas for living it out

Remember that while mobilizing can be calling others to God's global purposes, it can begin by simply inviting people to join a World Christian activity you are already doing.

01 What group of Christians are you already meeting with that you could

begin exposing to the World Christian lifestyle, i.e., Sunday school class, community group, Bible study?

02 Is there someone in that group you could partner with? Consider sharing your vision and goals, praying together, and working to mobilize that group together.

03 **Prayer**
Mobilizing people to pray for unreached peoples, internationals around you, and missionaries is an easy first step. How could you introduce world prayer into this group?

04 **Sending**
What are some ways you can mobilize your group to send and care for missionaries together?

05 **Welcoming**
If you haven't already started, how can you find and befriend someone of a different culture? How can you invite others from the group you are mobilizing to join you?

⏪ Review

World Christian Lifestyle Plan

Through each of the lessons in *Explore*, you've made personal applications based on what you've learned about God's Word, world, praying, sending, welcoming, going, and mobilizing. A holistic approach to learning encompasses our head, heart, and hands.

Head

01   What knowledge, understanding, and convictions have you gained by learning about the biblical basis of mission and the status of the world?

_____

_____

_____

Heart

02   What knowledge, understanding, and convictions have you gained by learning about the biblical basis of mission and the status of the world?

_____

_____

_____

Hands

How will you integrate what you've learned into your everyday life and put it in action? Take notes as you discuss these habits as a group.

03   **Pray**
     List some ways you can consistently pray for the nations and missionaries.

_____

_____

_____

04 **Send**

List some ways you can participate in sending a missionary. If it's an idea other than financial support, are there others that could do that with you?

05 **Welcome**

List some ways you can befriend or minister to people of other cultures and religious.

06 **Going**

Do you feel God may be leading you to go short term or long term? Who could you talk to about opportunities? If you don't know, check out thenations.us/go.

07 **Mobilizing**

What steps will you take to begin to expanding your World Christian influence among others?

08 **Learning**

It is also good to continue growing in your knowledge about God's Word, world, and work (there are some ideas and resources in the following pages under Next Steps on page 089). What could you do to learn more?

⧗ Pray

Now that you have a plan to play your role in God's global purpose, let's spend some time committing ourselves and our ways to God. Remember, God is even more excited about this than you are and will surely give you all that you need.

INTERCEDE

01   Father, give us power and courage to prioritize incorporating these practices into our lives.

02   Father, help us keep our minds and hearts focused on you so these practices don't become legalistic rituals, but remain our joyful participation in your global purpose.

03   Father, we pray that you would indeed make your name holy and exalted among all the peoples of the earth. We pray that your kingdom would come and your desires would happen on earth, among all peoples, the same way they happen in heaven.

Appendix
& Resources

Next Steps

- **Lead an *Explore* study yourself**

  In the same way someone invited you to go through *Explore*, you can invite others to join you, too. Grab some friends, maybe a coleader, and walk with them as they discover God's love for all the nations and how they can be involved! You can order copies of *Explore* and download our helpful leaders guide at vianations.org/explore.

- **Go deeper with *Explore* Resources**

  If your *Explore* study leader hasn't already lead you through some of the activities available online, consider asking him or her to do them with you. These are simple, real-world conversations you can have to go deeper into several of the topics this study brings up. vianations.org/exploreresources

Welcoming the Nations Among Us
`World Christian Series: Habit 03`

Our Father has always been a welcomer. He invites you to live a lifestyle prioritizing the mission of God through intentional cross-cultural relationships. vianations.org/welcoming

Mobilizing the Body of Christ
`World Christian Series: Habit 05`

Now that you are growing in the World Christian lifestyle, it's time to consider mobilizing others to do the same. This study is great whether you want to simply mobilize your community or make mobilization your career. vianations.org/mobilizing

Start living the World Christian lifestyle as a family

What would it look like to incorporate a heart for the nations into your parenting? *Parenting with a Global Vision* is a six-lesson study that will transform your parenting paradigm. vianations.org/pgv

- **Take a Perspectives Class**

  Experience God's heart for all peoples and encounter the momentum of the World Christian movement. Perspectives is a fifteen-lesson course that will open the eyes of your heart with a fresh understanding of God's unchanging purposes and why they're relevant to your life. perspectives.org

Biblical Basis of Missions

God's heart for the nations shines through in every book of the Bible, and it is His passion that drives our own. Below is a brief overview of the biblical basis of missions. If this sparks your interest, we suggest you commit to a 7- or 30-Day Challenge, available at vianations.org/exploreresources. Together, let's catch a glimpse of God's passion for all peoples to worship Him.

OLD TESTAMENT

The Beginning
- Genesis 1:28

Command to Noah
- Genesis 9:1

Tower of Babel
- Genesis 11:1–9

Promise to Abraham's Family
- Genesis 12:1–3, 26:4; 28:14

The Exodus
- Exodus 9:15–16, Joshua 4:23–24

Ten Commandments
- Deuteronomy 4:5–6

Solomon's Wisdom
- 1 Kings 4:34

The Temple
- 1 Kings 8:41–43

David and Goliath
- 1 Samuel 17:46

Shadrach, Meshach, Abednego
- Daniel 3:28–29

Daniel and the Lion's Den
- Daniel 6:25–27

Prophecy About Jesus
- Isaiah 49:6

The Psalms

- 2:8
- 9:11
- 18:49
- 22:27–28
- 45:17
- 46:10
- 47:1–9
- 57:9
- 66:1–8
- 67:1–7
- 72:8–11
- 77:13–14
- 86:9
- 96:1–13
- 98:1–9
- 99:1–3
- 105:1
- 108:1–5

NEW TESTAMENT

Testimony to All Nations
- Matthew 24:14
- Mark 13:10
- Mark 16:15
- Luke 24:46–47

The Great Commission
- Matthew 28:18–20

House of Prayer for All Nations
- Mark 11:17

Sent as Jesus Was
- John 20:21

Witnesses to the Ends of the Earth
- Acts 1:8

A Light to the Gentiles
- Acts 13:46–47

No Distinction Between Jew & Gentile
- Acts 15:7–19
- Ephesians 3:6–8

Obedience Among All Nations
- Romans 1:5
- Romans 16:25–27

Preach Where Christ Is Not Named
- Romans 15:15–21

All Nations Blessed
- Galatians 3:8

God Desires All People to Be Saved
- 1 Timothy 2:3–4

Propitiation for Sins of the World
- 1 John 2:2

Every Tribe, Tongue, & Nation
- Revelation 5:9–10
- Revelation 7:9–10

COMMIT TO A CHALLENGE vianations.org/exploreresources

7-Day Challenge
- Highlights five Bible passages per day for a week. These passages focus on God's heart for all people and how we can be involved.

30-Day Challenge
- Highlights five Bible passages per day for a month. This sampling of 150 passages give a deeper understanding that God's global plan and purpose runs from the beginning of Genesis, to the end of Revelation and everywhere in between.

Additional Resources

Mobilization Resources
- ViaNations.org

Prayer Resources
- OperationWorld.org
- GlobalPrayerDigest.org
- PrayerCast.com

Statistics and Resources
- TheNations.us
- AskAMissionary.com
- TheTravelingTeam.org

Books and Magazines
- Store.ViaNations.org
- MissionBooks.org
- MissionFrontiers.org

Share the Window

The Window is an excellent way to invite people to explore a World Christian lifestyle. In a simple sketch, you can share God's Word, God's world, and God's work. The Window helps you share the Bible verses you have memorized, as well as the THUMB acronym. Check out how it works.

The Window completed

GOD'S WORD	GOD'S WORLD	40
5 Bible Verses	5 Religion Blocs (THUMB)	
Gen. 12:1–3; Ps. 46:10; Is. 49:6; Matt. 28:19–20; & Rev. 7:9	Tribal, Hindu, Unreligious, Muslim, & Buddhist	
GOD'S WORK		
5 Habits	**?**	
Going, Sending, Welcoming, Mobilizing, & Praying		10

Sharing the Window

STEP 1

Transition: Start off by asking your friend if he or she has ever heard of the World Christian lifestyle or understands what it means to be a World Christian.

Action: Draw the Window diagram with four panes in the middle. Leave the diagram blank for now.

Explanation: Explain that by using this diagram, we can better understand God's global purpose and what our role is as followers of Christ.

STEP 2

Transition: Say, "But in order for us to understand God's global purposes and to join with Him in the most strategic way possible, there are three areas we need to understand. These three are: ..."

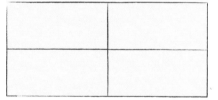

Action: Label the top left box "God's Word," the top right box "God's World," and the bottom left box "God's Work." Leave the bottom right box blank for now.

Explanation: Explain that World Christians are simply Christians who have a global perspective on their Christian life. They have come to understand these three areas: God's Word, God's world, and God's work, and they live their lives based on this.

STEP 3

Transition: Starting with God's Word, ask your friend if he or she knows any verses that deal with mission or with the nations. Write any of these verses somewhere to the side of the Window.

> **GOD'S WORD** ⟵
> 5 Bible Verses
>
> Gen. 12:1–3; Ps. 46:10; Is. 49:6;
> Matt. 28:19–20; & Rev. 7:9

Action: Now tell your friend that the Bible is full of verses about God's love for the nations, but we are going to focus on five. Write "5 Bible Verses" in the box labeled God's Word. Then list out: Gen. 12:1–3, Ps. 46:10, Is. 49:6, Matt. 28:19–20, and Rev. 7:9.

Explanation: Spend a few minutes going over the five verses, pausing to explain how each verse shows God's global purpose. It's good to have a Bible with you as you share, but we also encourage you to have the verses memorized.

STEP 4

Transition: "We just read that God desires to reach all nations and peoples with His gospel. In light of this, a World Christian needs know what the world looks like today and what people groups have not yet heard the gospel message. Currently, almost all unreached people are members of one of these five mega groups."

> **40**
>
> **GOD'S WORLD**
> 5 Religion Blocs (THUMB)
>
> Tribal, Hindu, Unreligious,
> Muslim, & Buddhist

Action: Write "5 Religion Blocs" and next to it the THUMB acronym in the box labeled "God's world." Say something like: "If you can remember your thumb, then you can remember 90 percent of the world's unreached people groups." You can also write the number "10" outside the bottom right corner of the diagram and the number "40" outside the top right corner. Use these two numbers to explain the 10/40 Window, the geographical area where most of the world's unreached live.

Explanation: Explain the five religion blocs: Tribal, Hindu, Unreligious, Muslim, and Buddhist. Explain to your friend that very little of the global church's attention is focused on these five groups — that they receive less than 10 percent of the church's missionary efforts and less than 0.1 percent of financial resources. Mention the ratio of Christian workers per million unreached (see page 020). For example, there are only two workers per 1 million Hindus. In contrast, explain how the majority of the global church's time, talent, and treasure go to reach places that are already strongly Christian. Make sure you explain the difference between the reached and unreached.

STEP 5

Transition: "In light of God's Word and the needs in God's world, World Christians are engaging in God's Work. And they do this by practicing the 5 Habits of a World Christian."

GOD'S WORK
5 Habits

Going, Sending, Welcoming, Mobilizing, & Praying

Action: Write "5 Habits" in the box labeled God's Work. Then list out the five habits: Praying, Sending, Welcoming, Going, and Mobilizing.

Explanation: Go through each of the habits, explaining what they mean. Ask your friend why we call these "habits" and not "choices." Explain that the purpose is to incorporate as many of these habits as possible into the rhythm of our lives, not just pick one out of obligation so we can we did our part in missions. Share what you are doing to live out a World Christian lifestyle and point your friend to opportunities to adopt similar habits.

STEP 6

Transition: "So far we have looked at God's Word and how he desires to reach all peoples. We've looked at God's world and have a better understanding of the task remaining. And we just looked at the 5 habits of a World Christian. Now it's time that we give an honest assessment of our own lives."

?

10

Action: In the last pane of the window draw a question mark.

Initiation: Ask your friend, "Now that we have briefly looked into this window to see God's Word, God's world, and God's work, would you like to learn more?" If your friend says "yes," give a few minutes to talk about what interests him or her. Afterward, use those interests to extend an invitation to some next steps, most likely to go through the *Explore* study with you. Explain how the *Explore* study helps people grow in the area that interests him or her, plus all the others as well. Schedule a day and time to begin *Explore* and then write it on the diagram. Let your friend keep the diagram.

CONCLUSION

Take a few minutes and pray together.

True/False Answer Key

Lesson 2, page 016: T, T, T, T, T, T, T, T, T, T

Lesson 3, page 028: F, T, T, T, T, T, F, T, T

Lesson 4, page 040: F, F, F, F, F, F, T

Lesson 5, page 052: F, T, T, F, T, T, T, F

Lesson 6, page 064: F, F, F, F, F, F, F, F

Lesson 7, page 076: F, T, F, F, F, T, F, T

Sources

All quotes at beginning of lessons used by permission from The Traveling Team. thetravelingteam.org

Statistics in "Fact Check" Section

- "The Task Remaining" by Ralph D. Winter and Bruce A. Koch, *Perspectives on the World Christian Movement, Reader*. 4th ed. William Carey Library, 2009, p.531–546.

- *Operation World. 7th ed.* by Jason Mandryk, Biblica Publishing, 2010, p.1, 6, 33, 447.

- The Gideons International, gideons.org

- Wycliffe Bible Translators, wycliffe.org

- Joshua Project, joshuaproject.net

"Read" Articles

Lesson 01   *God's Heart for the World* by Todd Ahrend, *Perspectives on the World Christian Movement, Reader*. 4th ed. William Carey Library, 2009, p.49.
Used by permission from The Traveling Team.
thetravelingteam.org

Lesson 02   *Those with No Access*, adapted from *The 10/40 Window* by Bryan Lee. Statistics have been updated from original article. 10/40 Window designations from Global Mapping International.
Used by permission from The Traveling Team.
thetravelingteam.org

"Pray" Section

Stories from Global Prayer Digest: globalprayerdigest.org
Statistics from Joshua Project: joshuaproject.net

Acknowledgments

A special thanks to the original authors and compilers, Andy K. and Joe M., and to subsequent editors, Christina G. and Titus H.

Endnotes

1   "The Story of His Glory" by Steven C. Hawthorne, *Perspectives on the World Christian Movement,* Reader. 4th ed. William Carey Library, 2009, p.59.

2   In every geographical-political nation, like India or Brazil, there are dozens to thousands of different people groups. These people groups can live in the same city, but have virtually no interaction with each other because of differences in language, customs, or religion. There are some Christians in every country, but that does not mean those Christians have easy access to every other people group in their country. In fact, sometimes there are almost insurmountable barriers between people groups living near each other. So, just because there is a church in among one people group in New Delhi, does not necessarily mean they can easily connect with another people group in New Delhi.

3   Statistics from Joshua Project, joshuaproject.net

4   Statistics from "The Task Remaining" by Ralph D. Winter and Bruce A. Koch, *Perspectives on the World Christian Movement*, Reader. 4th ed. William Carey Library, 2009, p.541.

5   Statistics from "The Task Remaining" by Ralph D. Winter and Bruce A. Koch, *Perspectives on the World Christian Movement*, Reader. 4th ed. William Carey Library, 2009, p.541.

6   Statistics from The Institute of International Education, Inc., iie.org

Notes

Pass it on.

Share what you've learned in *Explore* by starting a WORLD CHRISTIAN SERIES study today.

It's easy to lead a few friends, coworkers, or members of your church through the World Christian Series. Simply start with the reading, then work your way through the discussion questions.

Start with *Explore*, or go deeper on a particular World Christian Habit with *Welcoming* or *Mobilizing*.

→ vianations.org/wcseries

Introductory Study

Explore the World Christian Lifestyle